NEW BOOKS FOR NEW READ

Phyllis MacAdam, *General Editor*

Kentuckians Before Boone

A. Gwynn Henderson

THE UNIVERSITY PRESS OF KENTUCKY

For Narn and Dad, Lenape, and David

On the cover: At-Night, Flies-Alone, and their baby daughter return home after a walk.

The cover illustration and the drawings on pages 7, 31, and 32 are by Dr. Virginia Smith. The remaining illustrations are adaptations by Dr. Smith of drawings by Jimmy A. Railey depicted on the Kentucky Heritage Council's poster "Kentucky Before Boone." The photograph on page 55 is courtesy of Christopher A. Turnbow.

Copyright © 1992 by The University Press of Kentucky

Scholarly publisher for the Commonwealth,
serving Bellarmine College, Berea College, Centre
College of Kentucky, Eastern Kentucky University,
The Filson Club, Georgetown College, Kentucky
Historical Society, Kentucky State University,
Morehead State University, Murray State University,
Northern Kentucky University, Transylvania University,
University of Kentucky, University of Louisville,
and Western Kentucky University.

Editorial and Sales Offices: Lexington, Kentucky 40508-4008

Library of Congress Cataloging-in-Publication Data

Henderson, A. Gwynn.
    Kentuckians before Boone / A. Gwynn Henderson.
        p.   cm. — (New books for new readers)
    ISBN 0-8131-0908-6 (alk. paper)
    1. Fort Ancient culture—Kentucky.   Indians of North
America—Kentucky—History.   Indians of North America—
Kentucky—Social life and customs.   I. Title   II. Series.
E99.F7H46   1992
976.9'01—dc20   92-11161

Contents

Foreword

The New Books for New Readers project was made possible by funding from the National Endowment for the Humanities, the Kentucky Humanities Council, and the Scripps Howard Foundation through the *Kentucky Post*. The co-sponsorship and continuing assistance of the Kentucky Department for Libraries and Archives and the Kentucky Literacy Commission have been essential to our undertaking. We are also grateful for the advice and support provided to us by the University Press of Kentucky. All these agencies share our commitment to the important role that reading books should play in the lives of the people of our state, and their belief in this project has made it possible.

This Kentucky Bicentennial volume was made possible in part by the Kentucky Heritage Council (the State Historic Preservation Office). Heritage Council programs such as the National Register of Historic Places and the Archaeological Registry Program have collected information on over 40,000 important historic structures and archaeological sites. Through publications such as this, the Heritage Council is making information about Kentucky's rich cultural heritage accessible to all Kentuckians.

Because the printed word is a vital source of our commonwealth's heritage, we believe that books about our state's history and culture written for adult literacy students can convey information about the past to Kentucky citizens who might not otherwise have the opportunity to participate in our programs. We offer these books in the hope that, in content and by example, they will be of value to adult new readers.

Virginia G. Smith, Executive Director
Kentucky Humanities Council

Preface

A fascinating story lies beneath the feet of all Kentuckians. It is the story of prehistoric Kentucky.

I wanted to share with Kentucky's new adult readers some of the story as I understand it. So I wrote about Fishes-With-Hands and his family, who lived in central Kentucky in 1585, about 150 years before Daniel Boone was born.

I've drawn the information for this story from two different sources. One source is descriptions of Indian groups in the eastern United States made by Euroamerican traders and visitors and by people held captive by Indians. The other is information collected from archaeological sites in Kentucky, such as the Larkin site in Bourbon County, the Goolman site in Clark County, and the Hardin Village site in Greenup County.

I had another reason for writing this book. I wanted to learn how to write about Kentucky's prehistory for people who are not archaeologists. To be able to do this, I first had to picture clearly for my readers how these Indians lived, worked, and died. To my surprise and delight, I have found that I have drawn the picture of their lives much more clearly for myself.

I would like to thank the executive director of the Winchester/Clark County Literacy Council, Peggy Greenwald, and the new readers and their tutors who read and commented on this book as it was becoming: Jearl Arthur, Lamar Street, Tamara Flinchum, Pat Noel, Floyd Flinchum, Lula Holman, Paul Griffee, Jo Brennan, Mary Newkirk, and Betty D. Snowden. They suffered with me through the early chapters until I finally found "my voice," and their suggestions and questions have helped make the book better.

I would also like to thank the Kentucky Heritage Council for funding this project. This book represents another effort on the part of the Heritage Council to bring prehistory to the people of Kentucky.

I owe many thanks to my friends, archaeologists and regular people alike, who expressed interest in my book. They made suggestions and gave me other books to read. They also reviewed the final draft to make sure that I wrote "The Truth," at least as far as we know it. The outside reviewers' comments also were very helpful, and I thank them as well.

Finally, special thanks go to Phyllis, who gave me support and friendship, and to David, who's clearly more of an anthropologist than I am.

About the Author

A. Gwynn Henderson, a Delaware native, has always been interested in old things. At 13, she decided to become an archaeologist after reading a story about Pompeii in a book her parents gave her. She went on to get a bachelor's degree in anthropology from the University of Delaware in 1975 and to work on archaeological projects in Mexico, Tennessee, Kentucky, and Indiana.

Since graduating with a master's degree in anthropology from the University of Kentucky in 1982, the author has worked mainly for the University of Kentucky's Program for Cultural Resource Assessment. During her short stay at the Kentucky State Nature Preserves Commission, she developed the Kentucky Archaeological Registry Program, which encourages landowners to protect and preserve archaeological sites located on their land. Her research, carried out at sites in Kentucky and West Virginia, focuses on the pottery-making Indian cultures of the central Ohio Valley. The author is especially interested in the Fort Ancient Indians (the subject of this book), who lived in this area before the Euroamerican settlers arrived. She and her husband, also an archaeologist, have written several articles and reports about Fort Ancient sites in Kentucky.

Picture the Past

This book describes Indian life in central Kentucky before the settlers arrived. The story is fiction, but it is based on the facts as we know them today. We know that people we call Indians or Native Americans lived in central Kentucky for thousands of years. We know about them because we have found the things they left behind. The men and women described in this story were part of a group we now call the Fort Ancient People. Their way of life lasted for over 700 years. This story takes place about 150 years before Daniel Boone was born.

Now picture the past. Imagine looking across central Kentucky from a high place. It's a bright, cloudless day in late summer. The view is very clear. You can see for miles and miles in every direction. The year is 1585 . . .

To the Reader: When new words appear in this book for the first time, they are shown in *italics*. The new words are defined in a glossary on page 58.

The Natural World

Most of central Kentucky is covered in forest. Some of the oldest trees are so big that three people can't touch fingertips if they put their arms around a tree's trunk. Many kinds of trees grow in these forests. They are oak, chestnut, beech, black walnut, maple, yellow poplar, ash, sycamore, hickory, elm, hemlock, and pine.

Colorful flowers and many types of mushrooms grow in the forests and along the forest edge. Fruits and berries grow on thick vines, low bushes, and smaller trees. Nuts of all sorts also grow on trees.

Fires set by the Indians or by lightning have created grasslands in some spots. Early settlers called them "natural meadows," "barrens," or "glades." Only a few trees grow in these grasslands. They are oak, honey locust, hackberry, cherry, walnut, blue ash, pawpaw, and buckeye. Native grasses and clovers, however, grow thickly in the grasslands. There is blue stem, wild rye, and running buffalo clover.

In other places, native cane, a woody-stemmed grass like bamboo, grows 10 to 12 feet tall. Early settlers called these places "canebrakes." No trees grow here, only thick stands of native cane. These canebrakes stretch for miles and miles across the rolling hills.

Hundreds of freshwater and saltwater springs flow

in central Kentucky. Animals are attracted to these salt springs or "licks." They like to drink the salty water or lick the salt on the ground. The animals also eat the grass and clover nearby. Large areas of land around the largest licks, sometimes as much as 80 acres, are treeless. This is because herds of animals graze and trample the ground.

The rivers and streams flow freely. In the spring and after a big rain, they rise up over their banks, flooding the lands nearby. During dry times, even the Ohio River can be waded across. The water is so clear the Indians can see the rocks and shells on the bottom. Everywhere the water is good to drink.

The rich forests, grasslands, canebrakes, and waterways of central Kentucky provide food for the Indians and for many kinds of animals. The largest land animals are white-tailed deer, elk, bear, and mountain lion. Smaller animals also live in this region. They are opossum, raccoon, wolf, bobcat, dog, fox, beaver, skunk, mink, squirrel, mouse, groundhog, and rabbit.

The skies are filled with all sorts of birds, such as crows, woodpeckers, ducks, eagles, owls, hawks, passenger pigeons, and songbirds. Ground birds, such as wild turkeys and quail, live in the forests and grasslands.

Box turtles, snapping turtles, snakes, and frogs live near the rivers. Garfish, bass, bluegill, sunfish, minnows, and catfish swim in the clear streams and rivers. Freshwater mussels also live in the water.

The Indians use plants and animals for more than just food. Wood from the forests is used for cooking and for building houses and canoes. Cane and grasses are woven into baskets and mats. Using bone needles and animal gut, the Indians sew animal hides together for clothing. They also wear beads made of animal bone and shell.

The natural world supplies the clay and stone the Indians use to make pots and tools. They find clay along the riverbanks. Jars and bowls are molded from the clay.

The Indians use rocks for many kinds of tools. They find *chert*, sometimes called "flint," along the rivers. It is a brittle rock and breaks like glass. It can be black, gray, brown, or blue and can be striped or solid in color. The Indians make arrowheads, drills, scrapers, and knives out of chert.

The Indians travel outside central Kentucky or trade with their neighbors for other rocks. They use hand-sized pieces of granite (a very hard, spotted rock) as hammers. Sandstone is a gray rock with a rough surface like sandpaper. The Indians grind corn and sharpen sticks on *abraders* made of sandstone. Pipes and pendants are carved from a soft, red stone called pipestone.

The Indians' well-worn trails criss-cross their homeland, joining the many separate villages. These trails cross the main rivers where the water is shallow or where the rivers are narrow.

Trails formed by deer and elk connect the salt licks. Sometimes the Indians' trails follow the animal trails. These trails can be 10 to 100 feet wide. Because so many animals walk these trails, sometimes the trails are worn three feet deep into the ground.

The Warriors' Path is an important north-south Indian trail. It crosses the Ohio River in western Greenup County and swings west and south across central Kentucky. It passes through the mountains in eastern Kentucky and through the Cumberland Gap. The Warriors' Path connects Kentucky Indian villages with Indian villages in Ohio, eastern Tennessee, Georgia, and South Carolina.

The Indians know all about the forests and grasslands, the rivers and springs, the animals and fish, and the rocks and clay found in their homeland. They know which wood is best for burning and which is best for building. They know which plants are good to eat and which are good for making baskets. They know the habits of every animal, bird, and fish. They know which springs have salty water and which springs have fresh water. They know which chert makes the best arrowheads and which clay makes the best pottery. They know where the trails from their village will lead them and how far away the nearest villages are located.

The Indians' lives depend on their knowledge of the

natural world. They do not get this knowledge by going to school. They get it by watching and learning how everything works and by making mistakes. They get it by listening to stories told around the fire. In other words, they learn how to live in their world by simply living in it.

Summer Village

Picture in your mind's eye a cool late summer morning in prehistoric Kentucky. It's the kind of morning that signals fall is right around the corner. The sun rose just a short time ago. A thick mist is rising from the river, but it will soon be burned away. The smell of burning wood mixes with the odor of cooking corn, drying meat, tobacco smoke, and garbage.

The village is beginning to stir. Over 500 people live in this village. Their 25 rectangular, bark-covered houses are scattered along the river bank. Large trees stand next to some of the houses, shading them as the sun rises. Corn fields surround the village. Beyond the fields is the forest.

Since these people make their living mainly by farming, they built their village near fertile, well-drained soils. But they also fish and gather freshwater mussels. Over long distances they travel by canoe, and they need fresh water for drinking. For these reasons they also built their village along the river's edge.

The summer village.

Near the village center, one house is much larger than the others. It is the house of the village chief and his family. It serves as a meeting place for the village leaders, too. There they discuss politics, marriages, trade, and other important matters that touch their lives.

Next to the chief's house is the open area where the villagers hold important ceremonies. The earth is so hard that no grass grows there. It has been packed down by the hundreds of people who have danced there for the past five years. The women sweep this area clean of garbage and debris before and after each ceremony.

House size varies. The largest ones measure 70 by 30 feet, while the smallest ones measure 50 by 18 feet. The houses are not arranged in any regular pattern within the village. The doors are large pieces of elm bark or bearskin. There are no windows. Smoke curls upwards from the roofs of some houses. It is the smoke from last night's fire escaping through the central smoke hole in the roof.

Between 15 and 25 people live in each house and make up a household. Each household is made up of several families. The people of each household are most closely related to the people who live in the nearby houses. This is because they belong to the same clan. Several clans live in this village. The clans are known by animal names: Snake, Turtle, Raccoon, Turkey, Hawk, Deer.

Men cannot marry women of their own clan. When couples marry, the wife comes to live with her husband. When children are born, they belong to their father's clan. And when people die, they are buried in shallow graves in the clan's special burial area at the village edge.

Each house is surrounded by an open area that is mostly bare ground. This open area is largest in front of each house. The villagers do most of their work in this open area, except on the rainiest days.

Today is turning into a beautiful day. The sun has

burned the mist away. The river sparkles. A gentle breeze blows across the water into the village.

Although it is still early, most members of the nearest house are gathered in front of it. This is the home of Fishes-With-Hands, the brother of the village chief, and She-Who-Watches, his wife. Their two unmarried daughters and their youngest son live with them. So do their three married sons, their wives, and their nine children. The men and their children are members of the Raccoon clan. Their wives are members of the Hawk or Deer clan.

The women and older girls have already eaten and are busy with their household chores. The men and older boys discuss the upcoming harvest ceremony as they eat.

Most of their clothing is made of deerskin. The women wear wrap-around skirts, and the men wear short aprons or breechcloths. Their feet are bare. The women wear their dark hair long and braided. The men's hair is cut shoulder length. Most of the men wear headbands. One or two feathers are tied to a few of the older men's headbands. Everyone wears some kind of jewelry. Ornaments made from bone are tied into their hair. Around their necks hang pierced elk teeth, beads made of birds' wing-bones, or disk-shaped shell beads.

Flies-Alone, the wife of the eldest son, is working close to the front door of the house. She tends a stew pot that rests on a small mound of dirt in the center of the cooking fire. The stew is made from corn kernels,

9

beans, and squash boiled with strips of deer and elk meat, and chunks of squirrel. She stirs the stew with a long wooden spoon.

A short distance away lies her flat sandstone grinding slab. It has a wide groove down its center, worn down from much use. She kneels down next to the slab. Taking a hard stone in both hands, she bends forward over it. She begins to grind dried corn kernels into a coarse corn meal.

Corn is her people's main food. She and the other women of the village fix it in a number of different ways. This morning she will make a kind of bread by mixing boiled beans with corn meal. She will make this mixture into small cakes and then will bake these cakes under the ashes.

A large pot full of dried, whole corn kernels sits to one side of the fire. This corn is soaking in a mixture of wood ashes and water. Eventually the kernels will swell and burst from their skins. Then Flies-Alone will pound or grind the kernels into hominy meal.

Her sister-in-law, Rabbit-Catcher, and her almost-grown niece are working some distance from the house. They are making a new drying rack. As they work, their bracelets of bone and shell beads slide up and down on their arms. The women are building this rack from straight branches cut from young trees. Yesterday they stripped the bark from the branches. Today they are tying the branches together with cord made from slippery elm bark. When it is finished, they will set this rack, along with several others, around the drying fire.

Flies-Alone's other sister-in-law, High-Jumper, is working near the drying fire. She is preparing meat to hang on the racks. Yesterday, her eldest son brought part of a deer back to her from the hunt. One leg was roasted in the fire and eaten at once. Just before nightfall, she finished skinning the other leg. Now she is cutting the meat away from the bone and making thin strips. She will hang these strips of meat over the poles of the racks to dry.

An old woman steps out of the house. She is called She-Who-Watches, and she is Flies-Alone's mother-in-law. She squints into the sunshine. Her braided white hair shines in the morning sun. A shawl of woven silk grass covers her stooped shoulders. Around her ankles are strings of tiny shells. Her sons brought them back to her from their last trading trip. She pulls back the skin door of the house and hooks one corner back so the door stays open. Then she turns and goes back inside.

The house is dark. The sunlight that streams in through the door casts her shadow sharply on the floor. The floor is made of dirt, packed hard from being walked on by many feet.

Her shadow moves across the floor and falls on an inside wall. This wall divides her house into a small room and a much larger room. The household uses the

11

small room as a storage place and the larger room for sleeping.

Rabbit-Catcher makes a basket.

In the storage room, gourds and clay jars line the walls. Many hold dried corn from the early harvest. A few contain the last of the parched acorns from last winter or hickory nut oil. Several ropes of corn hang from the rafters. Small dried salt cakes, made at the nearby salt lick, are stacked in a corner. Other household items, such as baskets and fishing nets, hang from pegs along the walls. Dried bunches of smartweed and sumac branches also are tied to pegs. Smartweed is a peppery-tasting herb the women add to stews. The women use the leaves, berries, and stems of sumac in teas and medicines.

Chert river rocks are piled in one corner. Skin bags hold the tools her husband and sons use to make arrowheads and scrapers. The bags hang on pegs over the pile.

She-Who-Watches walks through the storage room into the larger sleeping room. A shaft of light from the smoke hole in the roof falls on the floor below. This light is filtered by the smoke rising from the central fireplace. The dim sunlight and the glow from the few remaining coals of last night's fire are the only source of light. Personal items hang from the rafters or from pegs along the walls.

The women of this household built their house in the spring about five years ago. That was when their people moved here from an old village located upstream.

The women chose small hickory or oak trees with straight trunks to use as posts for the framework. They peeled the bark off the tree trunks to keep worms and insects from eating into the posts. They sharpened the base of each post to a point with a chert knife. Then they hardened each post base in a fire.

Each post was pounded into a hole in the ground. Hundreds of tiny round pebbles, collected by the children from the river, were used to wedge the posts tightly into the ground. The pebbles helped to make the house framework sturdy. The women left openings three feet wide at the narrow ends of the house for the doorways. A doorway between the two rooms also was left at the end of the inside wall.

The women used branches from elm or ash trees to make the walls. These branches were woven in and out between the posts. They used this same kind of framework to make the roof.

Elm bark formed the outside walls and roof of their house. The women peeled the bark off large elm trees

13

and flattened it using small logs. Once the bark was flattened, they spread it on the framework. They held the bark in place on the framework by laying poles across it and tying these poles to the framework.

As with any house, this one needs to be kept up. So the women of the household repair it from time to time. Posts rot and have to be replaced. The roof will begin to leak and will have to be patched. In time, so many insects and field mice will live in the house that it will no longer be a comfortable home. At that time, it will have to be torn down and rebuilt.

The quiet, dark sleeping room has very little furniture. Benches line the walls. They are made from the trunks of small trees tied together with slippery elm cord. They are covered with bear and elk skins. The household uses these benches as seats, tables, or beds. Each family has its own area in the sleeping room where their members sleep and keep their personal belongings.

Shallow pits are located under the benches. The women dug these pits in the floor of the house to store dried food, such as berries, nuts, or corn. Valuable items used in ceremonies also are stored in these pits. Some of the pits are lined with grasses or bark and are covered with animal skin. The skin is stretched tightly to make it harder for mice to get into the food. It is held down with short wooden pegs.

She-Who-Watches searches under the bench closest

to the door for her broom made of long thick grasses. She sweeps up the loose ashes from the fireplace into a long wooden tray.

Outside once again, she stoops to pick up the pieces of a broken jar piled up next to the house. She greets Flies-Alone as she walks past her.

A pile of animal bones lies on the ground next to High-Jumper. These bones are left from preparing the deer meat for drying. She-Who-Watches gathers the bones up into her wooden tray, too. Then she walks around to the side of the house. She dumps the ashes, pieces of broken jar, and animal bones into a deep circular garbage pit.

On her way back, she checks the small, smoldering pits scattered around the outside of the house. They do not need more corn cobs. Mosquitoes and other biting insects are a real problem in the village. They are especially bad on warm, muggy summer nights. Smoke made by the smoldering corn cobs keeps some of the insects away. At the beginning of the summer, she and her two daughters dug these small smudge pits using pointed digging sticks. They filled the pits with shelled corn cobs and then set them on fire.

She-Who-Watches sits down slowly, cross-legged on a mat not far from Flies-Alone. A mound of clay is heaped up on a flat piece of bark near her knee. A small bowl of milky-colored water sits next to it.

She and her daughters-in-law brought clay home

from the clay bed along the river about a week ago. She got the clay ready for pot-making by cleaning out the small bits of rock and grass. To keep the pot from cracking when it is baked, she mixed in tiny pieces of burned, crushed freshwater mussel shells.

Before she begins to make the first pot of the day, she looks at the ones scattered around her work area, drying in the shade. The largest jars with narrow mouths will be used for storing food. Other large jars with wide mouths will be used for cooking.

The small bowls will be used at mealtime as personal serving dishes. On the rims of two bowls, she added clay otter heads for decoration. For the third one, she made a clay frog and stuck it to the outside as if it were looking down into the bowl.

She decides to make one more jar before she bakes this group of pots. Taking a handful of clay from the mound at her knee, she rolls a ball of clay between her palms. She presses the ball against her elbow to form a cup or shallow bowl. This is the base of the jar. She places it on a large curved piece of broken pottery. By doing this, she will be able to turn the jar as she forms its walls.

As she waits for the base of the jar to dry out slightly, she rolls three other balls of clay into long ropes. Then she coils each rope around and around on top of the jar base. She keeps her hands wet by dipping them in the bowl of water at her knee. She presses and smooths each coil into the one below. She works this way until she has built up the walls of the pot. Using her thumb and index finger, she shapes the lip of the jar.

Next she smacks the outside of the soft clay pot with a wooden paddle wrapped with cord made from silk grass. One hand holds the paddle while the other is inside the pot. Smacking the pot like this helps to join the clay coils firmly.

Now that she has made the jar, she thins and shapes its walls and smooths the inside surfaces with a mussel shell. She also smooths the jar neck on the outside but leaves the cord marks on the rest of the jar. She presses two wide, triangular strips of flattened clay onto the outside of the jar. These are its handles. With her index finger, she notches the lip of the jar. With a pointed stick, she decorates the jar neck. She makes the zig-zag design her mother and grandmother before her used to decorate pots.

After this last pot is made, it is time to build the fire in which she will bake her pots. When the coals are ready, she will clear out a spot in the middle of the fire. She will place all the pots she has made this week upside down in this spot. Then she will cover them with the hot coals. The heat from the coals will make her pots hard, watertight, and sturdy. The pots will come out ready to use. They will be dark gray or tan, with the tiny specks of white shell peeking through.

While She-Who-Watches is building the fire, her two daughters return from the river with elk bladder bags filled with water. They pour the water into large pots that stand near the cooking fire. As they pour, they talk about the return of their brothers, At-Night and Steals-Corn. Three weeks ago, the two men left with other men from the village on a trading trip to the south.

She-Who-Watches' youngest grandchildren, two small babies, are strapped to wooden boards that lean against the outside wall of the house. Each baby is wrapped in a woven rabbit-fur blanket. They begin to cry and fuss. Everyone speaks a little louder to be heard over the noise. As they work, the women talk about Masked-Eyes, a relative who is very ill. They wonder aloud if he will live to see this year's harvest ceremony.

A crash from behind the house makes everyone turn and look. The young boys from this household are racing around the village. They dodge in and out between the wooden drying racks. As they head for the open work area, they hop over the smoldering smudge pits and chase around their mothers and sisters. They are yelling and shouting to each other. Following close behind them are their three dogs, barking loudly.

The head of the household, Fishes-With-Hands, is sitting cross-legged on woven grass mats, eating from a clay bowl. Two of his sons and his oldest grandson stand around the cooking fire where the stew simmers. The men dip hunks of cornbread into the stew.

Three men from the Deer clan join the men who are eating. The Raccoon and Deer clans are in charge of the annual harvest ceremonies this year. The men from the Deer clan have come to discuss the ceremonies. They have brought their stone smoking pipes and skin bags filled with a mixture of tobacco and sumac leaves. Food is offered, and soon all the men are eating and talking, smoking and planning.

The younger men turn their heads to watch a group of women and young children of the Hawk clan leave the village. Some of the married women have babies strapped to their backs. But some of these women are still single and might make good wives.

This group is on its way to the fields. The women and older children carry mussel shell hoes and skin bags of dried food. The younger children carry empty baskets woven from hackberry bark, split cane, or grasses. This close to harvest, they cannot afford to have the almost-ripe corn eaten by birds, squirrels, raccoons, or deer before they have a chance to pick it. Some family members will stay in the fields day and night until harvest, to keep the animals away. One woman in the group calls out to the women working in front of Fishes-With-Hands' house to join them later in the day.

The women walk along the path, talking as their children scamper ahead. They walk past the fields of other clans to get to their own fields.

19

On their way back to the village, they will gather wild plants that grow along the way. They will put whatever they find into their baskets. It may be fruits or berries that are in season, or maybe mushrooms, grasses, leaves, or bark. The women will use some of these plants as food, eating them fresh or drying them for later use. Some they will add to their corn dishes as spices to give the bland corn more flavor. Others they will use in ceremonies or as herbs to heal the sick. And some they will use to make dyes to stain their baskets.

The village fields do not look like the fields of today where only single types of plants are grown. Everything is planted together: corn, beans, squash, gourds, sunflowers, and tobacco. The bleached trunks of large dead trees, with their craggy, leafless branches, also stand in the fields. They are too big for the men and boys to cut down with their stone axes.

Last spring, before the villagers prepared them for planting, the fields were a jumble of dead corn stalks. Bean and squash vines, and withered sunflower and tobacco plants littered the fields. The women, girls, and younger children pulled up the weeds in these older fields. They made small piles of what was left of last year's crops.

The men and boys cleared more forest for new fields. They used their stone axes to cut down the smaller trees. They stripped lower branches from the larger trees and cut a wide ring of bark from around the middle of the trunk. This killed the larger trees so that their leaves wouldn't shade the crops planted near them.

The men piled the younger trees, brush, weeds, and old crops against the larger trees. Then they set fire to the fields. The ashes from the fire serve as fertilizer.

Steals-Corn cuts down a tree with a stone ax.

When the fields were ready, the women planted the crops. Women of the same household worked together. They planted the early corn first, in hills spaced about four feet apart in rows spaced about three feet apart.

With a wooden stick sharpened to a point at one end, one woman dug a hole in the ground. Following after her, another dropped several kernels of corn into the hole and covered them up. In this way, the women of each household would plant their fields.

In a few weeks, the early corn would have grown several inches high. The women mounded up dirt around each cluster of young corn plants with their hoes. Then they planted their late corn and their beans, squash, and gourds.

Beans, squash, and gourds were planted in every

21

other corn hill. Bean vines climbed the corn stalks as they grew. Squash and gourd plants covered the ground at the base of the corn plants, growing over and down the hills. Between the rows of corn hills, the women planted sunflowers and tobacco.

The women tended the crops throughout the summer. They used their hoes to keep the weeds in check and hilled the corn plants again when they were knee-high. Three kinds of corn grew in their fields: flour or bread corn, flint or hominy corn, and popcorn. The corn plants were much smaller than the corn of today. Each plant produced only a few small ears.

The women planted two kinds of beans, and the sunflowers they grew had several flowers on each plant. Their tobacco was stronger and harsher than today's tobacco. The plants stood only about three and a half feet tall. The women never topped their tobacco plants. The men considered the tobacco flower to be the best part to smoke.

The children reach the fields first. They run into the fields, yelling and waving their arms. The squawking birds fly away in front of them.

One woman stoops to pick a gourd or two. She will dry the largest ones to use as containers, birdhouses, rattles, masks, and as floats for fishnets.

When most of the corn is ready to harvest, the women and older girls will bring larger baskets to the

Flies-Alone tends the
corn with her shell
hoe.

field. They will fill their baskets with the ripe ears and
carry the heavy baskets back to the village.

Some of the corn will be eaten fresh or "green,"
roasted in the fire in their husks. Some of the corn will
be dried and soaked to make hominy. The women of
each household will strip the dry corn kernels from the
ears. They will use their hands or a section of a deer
jaw that still has the teeth in it. This corn will be
stored in clay jars. Other corn will be braided into long
ropes for storage. The women will strip the husks away
from the ear and braid the husks together, leaving the
ears dangling.

Not all of the dry corn will be eaten around
household cooking fires in the village. Some will be
saved as seed corn to plant in the spring. Some will be
eaten around small campfires built by the village
traders during their six-week journey to the south.

Trade in Salt and Shell

On this bright summer afternoon, the trading party from the village is walking northward at a brisk pace. The travelers are in high spirits. The trading trip was a success. Every step they take brings them closer to home.

The twelve men walk in single file. They are strung out along the path like the shell beads on the necklaces they carry in their skin bags. The path they follow across this broad wooded ridgetop is little more than a narrow rut in the ground. It is one of many trails in this area that make up the Warriors' Path. Men from many villages have traveled this north-south path on summer trading trips for generations.

The oldest man, At-Night, is a nephew of the village chief. He walks at the head of the line because he has made this trip many times before. At-Night knows the best places to cross rivers and where the best springs are located. He also knows how long the trip should take, so he paces the group. His brother, Steals-Corn, brings up the rear many yards behind. Between them walk two members of each of the other village clans. They are fathers, brothers, sons, and nephews from the Snake, Turtle, Turkey, Hawk, and Deer clans.

Each traveler has a bow and quiver of arrows slung over one shoulder and a large skin bag over the other. Several small bags are tied to each man's belt. The large skin bags are filled with the items each man got in trade. They contain shell ornaments tucked carefully into grass padding. They also hold brightly colored bird feathers and the dried leaves of mayflower, a plant used to make a tea for the sick.

In some of the smaller bags are face paints, mixtures of bear grease and dry colors made from minerals or clay. The men apply these paints before entering and leaving their own village and the town of their southern trading partners.

Other small bags hold smoking pipes nestled into mixtures of tobacco and sumac leaves. Food, mainly dried corn and strips of dried deer meat, is also carried in the smaller bags. The wives of their southern trading partners refilled their food bags for the return trip. But by now, most of these bags are empty. The travelers are relying on animals they can kill along the way and on the plants, roots, and berries they find.

This is the first trading trip for the three youngest men. Months ago, they were picked by the village chief to go with their fathers on this trip. Being chosen brought honor to the young men and to their families. All three are used to traveling within their homeland on hunting and fishing trips. But until now, they had never traveled beyond the limits of their own people.

The three young men are familiar with the stories their fathers and grandfathers have told of past trading trips. But they never imagined the things they have seen on this six-week trip. First they saw the beauty of the land they call home. Then they visited one of the large towns of the southern people. It had a wide plaza and tall mounds made of earth. Mud-walled houses were surrounded by a wooden stockade. They also saw for themselves the strange clothes and heard the foreign languages of the southern peoples. They ate different foods at the homes of their trading partners.

These young men, their fathers, and the rest of their families spent several weeks preparing for this trip. The women mended moccasins and shirts, made new skin bags, and fixed dried food for the men to take. The men checked their bows and arrows and met in the chief's house to plan the trip. The chief told them how many shell ornaments they would need to bring back for the fall ceremonies.

The most important activities centered around preparing the trade items. The three main items were cakes of packed salt, tobacco, and dried flowers of the goldenrod that grows near the village. These are good items to trade because the men can carry them easily on their long journey.

Salt-making was a special activity. The villagers had to make the salt at salt licks scattered throughout their homeland. The best lick was located two days away from the village. When they made salt at this lick, they camped near it for several days.

Salt was made in two different ways, depending on

whether or not the waters at the salt licks flowed freely. At licks where no water flowed freely, the salt dried as a thin white crust on the dirt. Both men and women gathered up this salty soil with their hands or with shell scoops. They put it into baskets that looked like funnels: wide at the top and narrow at the bottom. They hung these baskets from a pole suspended across two upright posts.

They placed broad shallow clay pots, called salt pans, beneath each basket. The salt pans were made near the salt licks. The women pressed clay into large earthen basins or onto clay or wooden domes. Then the women built a fire to bake the pans to make them sturdy.

The men and women poured clear water they had hauled from a nearby stream through the baskets. The water washed the salt from the dirt, and the salty water collected in the pans. When the pans were full, they placed them on a fire to boil the water away.

At licks where the water flowed freely, the men and women placed the salt pans in basin-shaped holes in the ground or on slabs of stone. They carried the salty water from the lick to the salt pans in skin bags or clay jars. To speed the natural evaporation of the water, they heated rocks in nearby fires. Then they dropped the rocks into the pans. Or they built fires under the pans and boiled the water away.

Once the salt formed, they scraped it off the insides of the pans with shell spoons. They molded the salt into cakes in small wooden or clay bowls or in large leaves. These cakes weighed between two and three pounds. They brought the cakes back to the village to dry completely. Some of the dried salt cakes were stored in their houses to be used by their families. The rest were used for trading with the southern peoples. Before the trading party set out on their trip, the salt cakes were packed into large skin bags.

On the eve of the trip, the whole village feasted and danced in the open area near the chief's house. At a ceremony held in honor of the trading party, the village chief made a speech about each trader. In a prayer, the chief asked the good spirits to grant the traders a safe journey. He also asked for good hunting along the way and good luck in trading.

Early in the morning of the following day, the trading party set out on its six-week journey. The men left the village and took the path to the fields. They continued east past the fields for a mile or so, before turning south onto the Warriors' Path. Their destination was a large town in eastern Tennessee.

The men walked across the grasslands and through the forests of Kentucky. They crossed the Kentucky River and its small feeder streams. They walked through the foothills and climbed into the high country of the Appalachian Mountains. In the mountains, the trail followed the broadest ridgetops, dropping down into the valleys only at the best stream crossings.

After crossing the headwaters of the Cumberland River, the men crossed through the break in the mountains now known as Cumberland Gap. Then they turned southwest and followed the valleys of the Powell and Clinch rivers to one of the large towns of the southern people.

Following the customs of trade, the men of the trading party painted their faces before they reached the town. They entered through the main gate, and immediately the people inside tied their hands. The traders allowed their hands to be tied as well to prove that they would follow the customs of their trading partners.

Clan leaders took them to the home of the chief. It was located at the base of the large earth mound near the town center. Following custom, the chief invited them to eat with him and the other town elders. The hands of the visiting trading party were untied, and they ate everything offered, refusing nothing.

Dances and ceremonies to honor the visitors were held in the town. The feasting lasted a week. During the festivities, the visiting traders let their trading partners know what they brought to trade and what they wanted in return.

The actual trading took place toward the end of the week. It was like brothers giving gifts to brothers. They traded by bartering, offering one item for another, and they did not haggle over the value of the items they got. Because they spoke different languages, they used sign language or *interpreters*. Trading helped keep relations peaceful between their two peoples.

The salt the villagers brought to trade was highly prized because of its excellent quality. Their trading partners use some of this salt themselves during ceremonies. They trade the rest to the peoples living even further south whose lands do not have salt licks.

The villagers also brought their homegrown tobacco to trade. Their trading partners like its taste. They mix it with the tobacco they grow themselves.

The goldenrod that grows near their village does not grow near the town of their trading partners. It's a good item to trade because a beautiful yellow dye can be made from the dried flowers. Their trading partners' wives and daughters like the color.

In exchange for the salt, tobacco, and dried flowers, their southern trading partners gave the visiting villagers brightly colored bird feathers and dried mayflower leaves. They also gave them tiny seashells and *gorgets* made from larger seashells. The men can get the same bird feathers in their homeland, but the mayflower does not grow in their region. The tiny seashells and gorgets can only be gotten from their trading partners, who must trade for them with the peoples who live to the southeast.

The village traders make shell beads in the shape of

tiny disks from freshwater mussel shells collected from the river near their village. But the seashells and the shell gorgets they get from their southern trading partners are different. They are more important than the shell ornaments they make themselves, because they can only be gotten in trade with the southern people.

A circular shell gorget engraved with a rattlesnake.

Their southern trading partners trade the seashells both loose and already strung. Their women pierce the tiny seashells and string them together on necklaces, bracelets, or anklets. They are worn by almost everyone in the village and make good presents to family and clan members.

The shell gorgets are powerful symbols of manhood, wisdom, and success. They mark the most important men of the village and are given out only by the village chief. Men who have shown bravery and skill in hunting or in raiding their enemies are given gorgets. Men who have helped settle village disputes or who have foretold an important event also are given gorgets. The men wear their gorgets around their necks. When they die, their gorgets are buried with them.

The gorgets are either circular or are shaped like human faces. The circular ones have rattlesnakes or spiders etched on them. Those shaped like human faces have two holes drilled for eyes. Noses and mouths are carved out of the shell. Lightning bolts are etched on their faces, extending from their eyes down their cheeks. These designs are important religious

A shell gorget shaped like a human face.

symbols. The men consider a trading trip a success if they get many beautiful and well-made gorgets.

When the trading was completed, the men from the village got ready to leave. Their trading partners sponsored a final ceremony on the eve of their departure. The men from the village painted their faces. The village men and their southern trading partners danced and ate together for the last time.

Now the trading trip is almost over. The men have put 15 more miles behind them today. It is almost dusk and time to make camp near a small stream on the edge of the foothills. From their camp, they can look out across a beautiful sight. It is the forests and rolling grasslands of home.

Since it is a clear evening, the men decide to sleep in the open. One of the travelers, a member of the

Hawk clan, starts their campfire using his fire-making kit. It has a pointed stick of poplar, a little square piece of white oak, and dry wood chips.

The youngest member of the party shot two rabbits and caught a large rattlesnake today. He skins and guts the animals with his knife before he puts them on the fire to roast. Those men who still have strips of dried meat chew on the last pieces. They sit around the fire, talking about how the village will celebrate their return. At-Night sits apart, smoking some of the tobacco his trading partner gave him. It has been a good day.

Death

Some weeks have passed since the traders returned from their trip. This early fall day finds most of the village busy with harvest activities. The open space in front of each house is covered with ears of corn drying on mats in the warm afternoon sun. Mothers and daughters sit side by side near the drying corn. They are shelling kernels from already dried ears or braiding the husks into long corn ropes.

Other women are returning to the village from the fields. They carry large full baskets of freshly picked corn. They dump the ears of corn onto empty mats, then stop for a drink of cool water from the water jar. With so much corn to pick, they return at once to the fields. Near the council house, a group of men practice a dance. The harvest ceremony is less than two weeks away.

Ears of corn also dry in front of the house located next to Fishes-With-Hands' house, but no women are shelling corn or braiding corn ropes there. The house seems deserted except for the smoke rising from the cooking fire near the front door.

A young woman, looking drawn, tired, and sad, is leading an old woman toward this house. Bent over from the arthritis in her back, the old woman walks with a wooden cane in one hand. She carries a beaverskin bag in the other.

The old woman is Bright-Horn, a member of the Deer clan. She is a healer. As a child, the spirits came to her in a dream, calling her to this task. She learned to be a healer from her teacher, who was also a healer. But she also taught herself about certain plants.

During her long life, Bright-Horn has used her knowledge of healing, soothing, and pain-killing plants to cure her people's illnesses. She brews teas to stop stomach cramps and women's pain. She prepares dressings to draw infection from wounds. She uses cobwebs to stop bleeding and offers willow bark to help toothache and headache.

Many of Bright-Horn's cures cannot work without the aid of the good spirits. They are called to help when she sings the proper song or performs the proper ceremony. She shakes turtle shell rattles or beats a small drum when she sings her songs. She uses the hollow leg bones of a turkey to suck the evil spirits from the bodies of the sick. With a special chert knife, she makes small cuts on an arm or leg to allow sickness put there by the evil spirits to escape.

Bright-Horn has helped women in the village through difficult childbirth and has eased the suffering of the dying. Now she has been called to help this young woman's father, Masked-Eyes, a member of the Raccoon clan.

Masked-Eyes is one of the chief's cousins. He is a respected village elder, and he sits in council with the oldest men of the village. A good hunter and runner in his youth, he became known as a peacemaker later in life. He wears a shell gorget shaped like a human face as a sign of this ability.

Several times this summer, Bright-Horn has been led to his house. On her first visit, she made a series of short, deep cuts on Masked-Eyes' right arm with her knife while she sang a curing song. This treatment seemed to improve Masked-Eyes' health somewhat.

His visits to the village sweathouse seemed to help, too. The sweathouse is a tiny building located near the river. Large stones, heated very hot in a fire built near the sweathouse, are carried into it with wooden tongs. A sick person sits in the hot sweathouse and then, while still sweating, jumps into the river.

Bright-Horn was called to Masked-Eyes a second time after the village traders returned from their trading trip to the south. This time she brewed a tea for him. It was made from equal parts of the dried crushed mayflower leaf brought by the traders, strips of a local root, and crushed sumac berries. Masked-Eyes drank the tea, but he grew weaker. Each day it was harder for him to breathe and his coughing became worse. Masked-Eyes had the wasting disease (tuberculosis).

As the two women reach the sick man's house, the young woman steps forward. She pulls back the bearskin door and follows Bright-Horn inside.

The house is dark and quiet. The flames of a small fire in the center of the sleeping room cast shadows on the walls and ceiling. After their eyes adjust to the darkness, the two women see Masked-Eyes. He is lying naked on a bearskin-covered bench beyond the fire. Breathing takes all his strength. The young woman's mother and sister sit side-by-side on a nearby bench, singing in low tones. In the firelight, their eyes glitter, wet with tears.

Masked-Eyes' death is near and Bright-Horn can do little to help him. But to help his spirit leave his body, she conducts a short ceremony. She takes several small polished bones from her beaverskin bag and places them on his chest. She sings a drawing song that calls his spirit to leave his body through the bones on his chest. She shakes a gourd rattle slowly as she sings.

When she is finished, Bright-Horn takes the bones off the dying man's chest and wraps them in deerskin. She will purify the bones later so they can be used again. Bright-Horn leaves Masked-Eyes in the care of his family and finds her own way home.

Late in the evening, Masked-Eyes' youngest son comes to Bright-Horn's house with the news of his father's death. It is his last stop. He has walked from house to house telling the members of the Raccoon clan that Masked-Eyes is dead. Raccoon clan members, in turn, pass the news on to members of the other clans. Family and friends come to Masked-Eyes' house to weep and mourn with his wife and children.

It is her people's custom that the healer does not attend the mourning ceremonies of the dead. Bright-Horn's work is done. Now it is the mourners' time to work.

At dawn, four friends of Masked-Eyes, members of the Turtle clan, arrive at his house. Last night, these men were chosen to be the body handlers and grave diggers. The oldest will be the funeral leader. Members of the Raccoon clan cannot do these jobs, because they are of the same clan as Masked-Eyes.

After eating corn stew prepared by Masked-Eyes' wife, the four men wash the body and dress it in new clothes. They paint the face with lightning bolts like those etched on Masked-Eyes' shell gorget. They place this gorget, awarded so many years ago, carefully on the chest. Then they wrap the body in a deerskin and lay it on a bench inside the house. The body will stay in this place for two days.

During these two days, the women of the Raccoon clan cook large amounts of food for the mourning feast. The four men of the Turtle clan spend this time preparing the grave. It is located not far from the edge of the village where the other members of the Raccoon clan are buried.

Using digging sticks and hoes, the men of the Turtle clan dig a shallow pit. With their hands, they scoop up the loose dirt and pile it beside the pit. They also look for slabs of limestone rock in the cornfields and along the riverbank. They carry the rocks to the pit and stack them in a small pile next to it. Some of the limestone slabs they set on edge to line the walls of the entire pit with rock. They will use the other stones to cover the body.

On the third day after Masked-Eyes' death, all of his relatives gather outside his house. The four men of the Turtle clan arrive. The crowd parts as the four men walk to the house. They disappear inside for a moment, then reappear carrying the deerskin-wrapped body on their shoulders. Members of Masked-Eyes' household and members of the Raccoon clan follow after them. They, in turn, are followed by members of the other clans.

Masked-Eyes' body is taken directly to the freshly dug grave. The four men lay the body in the grave on its back with the head to the west. They place Masked-Eyes' favorite bow and a single arrow along his right side. They put his favorite pipestone smoking pipe next to his head.

Once the body is in the grave, the funeral leader takes his place at Masked-Eyes' head. He

The last limestone slab is placed over the body of Masked-Eyes.

holds a small bowl containing tobacco. One by one the members of the funeral procession take a small amount of tobacco from the bowl. Walking around the grave from east to west, each person sprinkles tobacco on the body. In low tones, they ask that Masked-Eyes' spirit not look back to earth or think about the friends that remain behind. They ask the spirit to follow the way set out for the dead and not trouble his family and friends.

After the last person has sprinkled tobacco on the body, the men of the Turtle clan choose several limestone slabs from the stack near the grave. They fit them over the body, covering it completely. The mourners then return to Masked-Eyes' house. They will eat the feast that has been prepared by the women of the Raccoon clan.

When most of the mourners have finished eating, Fishes-With-Hands stands up and gives a speech. He talks about his cousin's life and his deeds. He asks the mourners to forget their loss and reminds them that death awaits them all. He gives away Masked-Eyes' personal belongings to his Raccoon clan relatives and to the four men of the Turtle clan.

On the twelfth day of mourning, a ritual feast is eaten at the graveside. This feast marks the end of the mourning period for all of Masked-Eyes' relatives except his wife. It is attended by only Masked-Eyes' closest family members and the four men of the Turtle clan.

The men build a ritual fire near the grave. Over this fire they cook a stew of shelled corn and beans in a jar made for this purpose. All of the mourners eat a little bit of this stew, using a special spoon made from a mussel shell.

After the last person has had some stew, the men of the Turtle clan cover the grave with another layer of limestone slabs. The funeral leader scatters wood and ashes from the ritual fire across the stones. Then he throws the jar on the limestone slabs, breaking it. He makes a speech, saying that with this act, the bonds of Masked-Eyes' spirit with the living are broken.

The men of the Turtle clan throw dirt over the stones and set painted sticks in the ground at either end of the grave to mark its location. Then, the funeral leader declares an end to the mourning period for all except Masked-Eyes' wife.

With the death ceremony completed, the group

walks back into the village. The mourners go directly
home to wash, oil, and comb their hair. This ritual
cleaning allows them to take up the activities of normal
life again.

Masked-Eyes' wife will mourn for 12 months. She
will wear the same clothes she wore the day Masked-
Eyes died, even though they will become worn and
dirty. She will not paint her face, wear any jewelry, or
wash her face and hands. At the end of the twelve
months, Masked-Eyes' closest blood relative will wash
her and dress her in new clothes and jewelry. At a
special feast, Masked-Eyes' wife will end her
mourning, and she will be free to marry again.

Winter Camp

The harvest was a good one. The women have shelled
bushels of corn and stored it away. The tobacco hangs
in bunches from the rafters of every house. The
marriage and harvest ceremonies have been danced for
the year, so most of the villagers have moved to their
winter hunting camps.

The village is almost deserted. The elderly and
those too sick to travel have stayed behind. So have
the smallest children and their mothers, and a few men.
The women will care for the children, the sick, and
elderly, while the men will hunt for them all.

This late fall day in 1585 is quite different from the beautiful summer day in the village over three months ago. The skies are gray. Dusk is near and it feels like rain. A chilly wind blows through the tops of the trees surrounding the camp and rustles the leaves on the ground.

This camp is one of many built by the Raccoon clan. It is located four days' journey or about fifty miles away from the village. It is built near the head of a small stream, tucked into a narrow valley in a small opening in the woods. Twenty people, all members of Fishes-With-Hands' household, live in this camp. It is made up of three small, oval, bark-covered huts arranged around a larger rectangular bark-covered building. This central building looks much like the village houses.

Trampled grass surrounds each hut. The grass already is worn away in a large open area in front of the central building. The daily activities for the whole camp take place here. The cooking fire for the camp is located near the doorway of the central building in this open area.

The women built the huts and central building much like they built their houses in the village. But they did not make them with as much care, because they will only use them for this season.

None of the structures have any windows, and only the central building has a real doorway. The door is made from bark or skin like the doors on the village houses. All four structures have smoke holes in their roofs. Smoke billows out of the hole in the roof of the central building and from one hut.

Only the women and children are in the hunting camp tonight. Two days ago, At-Night returned to camp with the news that he and Steals-Corn had killed two deer and a bear. Lacking pack animals for hauling, the two men needed their family's help to carry all the meat back. After a quick bite of roasted deer, Fishes-With-Hands, At-Night's father, his brothers, and his two sons left camp.

Several days ago, before At-Night and Steals-Corn left on their hunting trip, they put their weapons in order. They checked their bows and repaired their old arrows. They also made new arrows to replace the ones that had been broken or lost on previous hunts.

The men did their work in the large open area in front of the central building. They spread out all the tools and materials they needed on the ground. This included chert and antler for the arrowheads, native cane and seasoned hickory shafts for the arrows, and turkey and hawk feathers for the *fletching*. Then they sat down on bearskins and began to work. Their *knapping* tools were laid out next to them.

On a hunting trip, the men often shoot many kinds of game. So each man made several kinds of arrows. The arrows they made for shooting small game, such as beaver, bobcats, and groundhogs, were only sharpened shafts of hickory wood. Some weeks before,

Steals-Corn had scraped the bark off thin hickory branches. He had used a multi-purpose chert scraper to do this. It was shaped like a teardrop and *socketed* into a wooden handle. Both men finished this kind of arrow by hardening the sharpened tips in the fire.

Steals-Corn makes a chert tool.

The arrows the men use to shoot larger game, such as deer, bear, and elk, have native cane or hickory wood shafts. They are tipped with arrowheads made of chert or antler. To make chert arrowheads, the men used round, hand-sized hammers made of granite to chip off pieces of chert from larger chert rocks. They formed the general shape of the arrowheads from the smaller pieces using deer antler or wooden tools. The arrowheads were small triangles no longer than two inches. They finished the arrowheads with deer antler tines, the tips blunted from use. Tiny pieces of chert were removed from the nearly complete points, which gave the arrowheads very sharp edges. Steals-Corn, the best knapper in camp, could make a chert arrowhead in less than 10 minutes.

The men also made arrowheads out of deer antler

tines. Each man made a deep cut all around the antler shaft about two inches from its tip. Then they snapped the antler tines off cleanly at the cut. Any ragged edges were worn away by rubbing the base of the point on an abrader made of sandstone. The men removed the soft insides from the base of the point where the arrow shaft would fit. They finished the antler arrowheads by shaving them with a knife or rubbing them on the abrader to sharpen the points.

Each man attached his chert arrowheads to the shafts by inserting the base of the arrowhead into a notch in the tip of the shaft. The point was held in place by deer gut strips wrapped around the tip of the shaft or with a glue made from boiled deer antler. For the antler arrowheads, the men fit the shafts into the hollowed-out bases. The antler arrowheads were held firmly on the shaft with glue. Each arrow was finished by binding two or three large turkey or hawk feathers as fletching to the opposite end using either gut or deer antler glue.

With their weapons in good working order, the two brothers were ready to hunt. They took some food with them, but they also would eat what they could hunt along the way. They tucked their axes into their belts, bid their families goodbye, and left on the hunting trip with their dogs.

Back at the camp, the women are hurrying to finish their daily chores before night falls. This evening, although it is chilly, they work together outside in the open area. Later in the winter, when it becomes very cold, they will move their work inside. The members of the hunting camp also will cook, eat, and socialize in the larger central building when it becomes too cold outside. The head of the household uses the larger central building for sleeping, too. The other members of the group use the oval huts for sleeping.

She-Who-Watches and her two daughters are singing as they crack hickory nuts on a pitted sandstone rock near the door of the central building. An almost full clay jar of thick corn soup mixed with chunks of wild turkey meat simmers on the fire.

Cracking hickory nuts.

A huge pile of unshelled nuts is mounded up beside each woman. They are the results of a successful day of gathering. The women are cracking the nuts to make the oil they will use for cooking throughout the year. Each one holds a heavy stone in one hand. They place the nuts in shallow pits on flat sandstone rocks. They smash each nut and then gather up nut shells and nut meats into baskets that sit between them. When the baskets are filled, the women will empty them into a large jar filled with boiling water.

The nut shells will eventually sink to the bottom of

the pot and the milky nut oil will rise to the top. Then one of the women will skim the oil off and pour it into clay storage jars.

Flies-Alone is just about finished softening a deerhide with a wooden paddle. At-Night shot the deer six days ago while he was returning to camp from checking his traps. Every winter he sets several traps some distance from camp.

Hickory nut collecting in the woods.

These traps are made from logs and saplings. He catches small, fur-bearing animals like mink or beaver in them.

Flies-Alone skinned and butchered the deer the day At-Night returned. Her young daughters watched her, learning as she worked. First she tied the deer's hind legs to the lower limb of a nearby tree with strong cord. It was easier to butcher hanging up this way. Using a chert knife, she first cut the soft belly of the deer down the middle and removed the internal organs. She cut the hide from around each leg above the foot and around the base of the antlers. Then she skinned the deer. Starting at the rump, she pulled the hide away from the carcass until it was completely skinned. She folded up the hide for tanning later.

Next Flies-Alone butchered the deer. Still using her knife, she cut the front legs from the main part of the body and cut each one into three parts at the joints. She split the trunk of the deer in half along the backbone and cut each half into three parts. This left each hind leg still hanging from the branch. She cut each one into two parts.

With a stone axe, she chopped into the skull to remove the brains. She roughly hacked the antlers from the skull with her knife. She removed the lower jaw by smashing it at the joint, and she cut out the tongue. She saved certain bones (the lower jaw, ribs, leg bones, and toe bones) and the antlers from the deer. These would be made into tools and jewelry. The whole camp ate the animal, which she roasted in the fire after she was finished.

Five days ago, Flies-Alone began to tan the hide. First she scraped away the flesh on the inside of the hide. For this, she used a chert scraper similar to the ones the men used to smooth arrow shafts. She took care not to cut any holes in the skin.

Next, she soaked the hide for three days in a wooden vat filled with water. She scraped away any remaining flesh, then stretched the hide tight on a wooden frame. The hair was pulled away from the hide using a scraper. This was a long, hard job because she had to be careful not to cut the damp skin.

Flies-Alone prepares a hide.

After pulling away the hair, she worked a mixture of deer brains, ashes, and water into the other side of the hide. She worked and worked the hide with a wooden paddle until it was softened.

Tomorrow Flies-Alone will put the finishing touches on the hide by smoking it over a fire. She will roll the hide into the shape of a cylinder. Then she will hang it from a frame over a fire she will build in a pit near the camp. The smoke and heat will rise up from the pit through the cylinder. This will turn the hide a golden brown and will keep it soft even when it gets wet. When the hide is done on one side, she will unroll it and then roll it in the opposite direction and smoke it again. After she has tanned several hides in this way, she and the other women will be able to make new clothing, like belts, capes, shirts, skirts, leggings, and moccasins. Other items, such as drumheads and bags, also will be made from the tanned hides.

Flies-Alone's two sisters-in-law are smashing the

leg bones of an elk butchered several days ago. High-Jumper puts her bone fragments into another pot that is cooking on the fire. Cooking the smashed bones makes bone grease.

Rabbit-Catcher selects a splintered bone fragment to make a sharp pointed tool, called an awl. She sharpens the point of the bone fragment by rubbing it across a sandstone abrader.

Rabbit-Catcher and the other women in her family will use awls to make clothing and other items they need. First, they will use knives to cut pieces from the tanned hides. Next, they will use the awls to punch holes in the pieces. And finally, with fishbone needles threaded with animal gut, they will sew the pieces into clothing, bags, moccasins, and the other items they need.

Hearing noise from the closest hut, Rabbit-Catcher stops sharpening the awl and walks over to the hut. Pulling aside a bark strip, she looks in on her children and their cousins. Bearskin robes are spread on the packed dirt floor across the entire hut. Unlike the village houses, these huts do not have inside walls, benches, or shallow pits. There is only a central fireplace. The children are lying head to toe around the fireplace, covered with bearskin robes, but they are still awake. Rabbit-Catcher tells the children to hush and to go to sleep.

She-Who-Watches and her daughters begin to sing their song again. Flies-Alone, High-Jumper, and

Rabbit-Catcher join in. As they end the song for a third time, a noise from the woods stops them.

The men and boys are returning to camp loaded down with meat. In the fading light, they set the meat on the ground in front of the central building. Hands and backsides are turned to the fire for warmth. The women give corn soup in wooden bowls to the cold, tired travelers. The "sleeping" children join their relatives around the fire.

As the men eat, sitting around the fire, At-Night and Steals-Corn tell their stories of animals missed and of animals shot. They tell of hiding in the tall grasses downwind of the deer and stalking them slowly and silently until they moved within range. They drew their bows. Then on At-Night's signal, they let their arrows fly, shooting several deer at close range.

They were lucky to find the bear. One of the dogs scented it first. Then almost immediately, Steals-Corn noticed the scratch marks on a tree trunk. Looking up, he spotted the bear hole.

At-Night cut down a small tree with his axe and leaned it next to the tree with the bear hole in it. The brothers argued over who would climb the tree to disturb the bear. Finally Steals-Corn agreed to do it,

At-Night prepares to shoot the bear.

51

but he complained all the way up the tree. He got the bear's attention by hollering and shouting. When it appeared, At-Night shot it with one well-placed arrow.

As night falls, most of the household gets ready to go to bed. Each family walks to its separate hut. She-Who-Watches and her children go to the central building to sleep because Fishes-With-Hands is the head of the household. As in the oval huts, a central fireplace is built on its dirt floor.

Fishes-With-Hands and his two grandsons stay seated around the fire, talking, long after the others have gone to bed. The young men are still too excited with the household's good fortune to sleep. They ask their grandfather about other successful hunts, and he relates the stories from years past. As it gets later, the old man's stories turn to the deeds of relatives, either long dead or more recently passed away, and to the Creator, Our Grandmother, and Cloudy Boy who watch over their people.

To Step Back in Time . . .

The story of Fishes-With-Hands and his family shows that our lives are different in many ways from the lives of *prehistoric* Kentuckians. We lack their clear rivers, fresh food, and slower-paced life, while they lacked our electricity, cars, and grocery stores. But our ways of life also have much in common. We share the importance of family and home, the need to work for a living, the excitement of travel, the sadness of death, and the circle of the seasons.

Although their way of life vanished over 200 years ago, the Fort Ancient People can live again in our imagination when we see the things they left behind. To step back in time, all you need to do is walk across plowed fields on almost any farm in Kentucky. You can find the places where Indians once lived.

Today these places are called *archaeological sites*. And the artifacts, the remains of things that the Indians made and used and ate, are still there. There are arrowheads, broken pots, bone beads, shell spoons, stone axes, pieces of animal bone, and burned beans and corn cobs. Traces of the Indians' houses, trash pits, fireplaces, and burials are still there, too.

Every archaeological site is like a time capsule. It has a story to tell about the past. The shape, color, and size of each artifact is part of the story. So, too, are the traces of houses left in the soil and the remains of trash that was thrown outside.

But it takes more than just a single artifact or house to tell the story. Scientists must study where each artifact is found and what types of artifacts are found with it. Most important of all, they must read the patterns of the artifacts at sites.

Archaeologists are scientists who study these time capsules to learn about past Indian lifeways. They locate sites by walking plowed fields and by talking to farmers. After they find a site, they describe it and record it on maps. Often, they dig up, or excavate, parts of sites to learn more about the past.

Archaeologists excavate in a slow, careful, and organized way. They use shovels and trowels, spoons, paint brushes, and wire screens. Care is very important. Once dug up, the artifacts never can be put back in exactly the same way. Often, they are all that is left of a past way of life.

The holes archaeologists dig are square or rectangular. Holes shaped like this make it easier to record what the Indians left behind. Archaeologists dig the dirt out in thin layers. They find artifacts by screening the dirt. They keep the artifacts from the top layers separated from the ones at the bottom. This helps archaeologists read the patterns of the artifacts. The location of every artifact, house, trash pit, and burial also is recorded. Even samples of the dirt are

An archaeologist draws a map at the Goolman site in
Clark County.

saved. Archaeologists draw maps, write notes, and take
photographs of everything they find.

After the *excavation* is finished, everything is taken
to the laboratory. The photographs, maps, and notes
are studied. The artifacts are washed, sorted, and
studied for the patterns they can show. Computers help
archaeologists explain the patterns they find. In this
way, archaeologists reconstruct how the Indians lived.

The shapes of the arrowheads archaeologists collect
from a site tell them when the Indians lived there and for
how long. By studying the animal bones and pieces of
burned plants, they learn about what the people ate.
They can figure out how many people lived at a site by
counting how many houses they find. They learn about

the peoples' beliefs by studying how their dead were buried.

Archaeologists also learn about the Indians in another important way. Because the Indians did not write, archaeologists cannot read about their ways of life in their own words. But archaeologists can read about Indian life in the journals, diaries, and letters of early *Euroamerican* explorers, traders, and settlers. These writings, like the sites, are time capsules. Archaeologists discover descriptions of the Indians' ways of life in the books and maps held in libraries. They compare these descriptions with the artifact patterns they find at the sites.

Learning how the Indians lived isn't easy. As with an old puzzle, some pieces are always missing. The patterns are never complete. Archaeologists must work like detectives searching for clues.

Here is an example of what archaeologists face. Think about the artifacts you have in your home. Are your dishes fancy or plain? Do you have cookbooks and newspapers? Do you have a small black and white television, or is it a big color TV set? Do you own many pairs of shoes or just a few? Then think of how you use these artifacts in your home. Do you use the TV in a special room? Are the cookbooks in the kitchen and the newspapers in the living room? Where do you keep your dishes and your shoes?

Now imagine that your home has burned down.

You have moved away. Hundreds of years later, archaeologists return to the spot where your home once stood. Nothing can be seen above the ground. The spot is covered by grass and weeds. The dishes are broken and burned black. The cookbooks and newspapers burned up in the fire, along with all the other artifacts made from paper or cloth. Television parts are scattered everywhere. Only two burned shoe heels are left. This is all that remains of your home.

Several people in your hometown kept diaries while you lived in your home. Their children gave these diaries to the town library. These diaries tell what life was like back then. Now what can be said about how you lived? These are the puzzles archaeologists must solve.

Archaeologists have been at work in Kentucky for many years. They have excavated many sites and read many books in their search to learn about the Indians. State agencies, private groups, interested people, and new laws protect some of Kentucky's archaeological sites. You can help, too, by reporting site damage to archaeologists. By working together, we can make sure that the most important ones are saved for the future. In this way, we will be able to keep on learning about the Indians' ways of life.

Glossary of New Words

abrader - a rock made of sandstone that is used like sandpaper

archaeological site - a place where Indians once lived

archaeologist - a person who studies archaeological sites, artifacts, and artifact patterns to learn about the Indians' way of life

artifact - anything the Indians made or used, as well as the remains of what they ate

chert - a brittle rock that breaks like glass; also called flint

Euroamerican - an American whose ancestors came from Europe

excavation - digging, drawing maps, and taking notes and photographs at a site to get information about the Indians

fletching - the two or three feathers glued or tied onto the end of an arrow shaft

gorget - an ornament made from shell that is worn around the neck

interpreter - a person who can speak two languages well enough to help people who speak different languages to talk to each other

knapping - making a stone tool by knocking chips off a chert rock

prehistoric - a period of time in the past for which there is no written record

socketed - jammed or wedged into a wooden or antler handle

58